my first 7days in heaven

by
Andy Smith

my first 7days in heaven

Copyright © 2011
Vision Publishing
Ramona, CA 92065

All rights in this book are reserved world-wide.
No part of the book may be reproduced in any manner whatsoever without written permission of the author except in brief quotations embodied in critical articles of reviews.

ISBN: 978-1-61529-020-8

For information on reordering please contact:

Vision Publishing
1115 D Street
Ramona, CA 92065
1-800-9-VISION
www.visionpublishingservices.com

To my daughters
Tracy, KellyRae & Rosemary
who have made my life
Heaven on Earth

Create a great Heaven

Andy Smith

Create a Great Harvest

Table of Contents

Preface 7
Disclaimer 11
Indoctrination 13
First Day 31
Day Two 43
Day Three 53
Day Four 63
Day Five 77
Day Six 93
Day Seven 107
Day Eight a bonus day 113
Day Eight 115
Planning Your Heaven 127
Challenge 133
My Best Day in Heaven 133

Preface

I've said it before and I'm going to say it again. For a creative writer, you only need two words to get your adventure started... ***what if.*** Nothing gets the creative juices flowing better than these two simple words. *MY FIRST SEVEN DAYS IN HEAVEN* is a great example of the wonderful world of what ifs.

I had a dream. I don't put a lot of stock in dreams. I've always felt that dreams were just God's way of entertaining us while we're waiting to wake up. I never think about my dreams. I never analyze my dreams. I'm likely not to be able to tell you a thing about my dreams after my first cup of coffee.

But this was just one of those dreams were you wake up startled saying, "Wow ... that was weird."

I dreamed that I died and ended up in this holding room where this guy was going over everybody's name from a big book he was looking at. He passed out a sheet of paper with a bunch of lines on it and the words... *TODAY, I'M GOING TO* ... He explained that our Guardian Angel will explain the whole thing to us in the next room.

And that's when I woke up.

After my first cup of coffee, my two favorite words began to do their magic. I started running the 'what ifs' all over this dream and before my second cup of coffee, I was heading for my computer. I was having way too much fun with this idea to let it get away from me, so I started writing. I became obsessed with the whole idea and all the possibilities that came with every new adventure.

I have no idea if anyone will appreciate this piece of work. I've written many stories in my time, but this one is clearly the most fun I've had as a creative writer. With each day, I had to create new rules for Heaven that would make Heaven make sense. And once I got all those rules figured out, it simply became a fun adventure in living out my fantasies.

You may not get my first seven days in Heaven, but I'm hoping that you at least get the rules and start thinking what your first seven days in Heaven might be. That's what makes *what if* such a fun journey for us all.

The author

TODAY, I'M GOING TO --

Andrew Damien Smith

Disclaimer

Please take note of the fact that I am not a theologian, I am not a Bible scholar, and quite frankly doing a bunch of research bores the hell out of me. If you are one of those religious people who feel the need to scour over this story to prove through exhaustive biblical references that my Heaven is unlikely to be anywhere near accurate, it will only prove that you are a bigger idiot than I.

I like my Heaven, and I do think that my Heaven makes sense. It takes the basic hopes that we all have when we think about Heaven ... it is eternity with no time limits... it gives you the opportunity to be with those you love doing the things you love to do - with people still living on Earth as well as those who have gone before you ... and it does so without any consequences or negative outcomes.

As a religious man, I found myself going to church while I was writing this and smiling from ear to ear as I sat there contemplating my story. I realized that my Heaven is at its very least a worse-case scenario. I am certain that God's Heaven is much better than what I have come up with here ... and that to me is very exciting.

Indoctrination

I remember going into this room. There were a lot of people there. All different kinds of people ... different ethnic, styles and ages - though there obviously was no one under the age of thirty or so. Everyone seemed friendly, though a bit confused.

I took a seat and there was a man standing in front of a platform with a big book lying open. He seamed to be reading the book and paid little attention to those of us coming in and finding our seats.

It was a quiet, peaceful atmosphere. Everyone seemed to be as confused as I was, not knowing where we were or what was going to happen next. But as we all settled in, the man looked up and seeing that we were all ready, began to talk.

"Welcome. I am the keeper of the Book of Eternity. I will be brief in my comments as you will get a full explanation when you leave here of what to expect moving forward.

"First, you must understand that when you crossed over to this side, your soul, or heart if you will, went through what we call the wash. Everything that was negative in your life on Earth was washed away. You have no memory of pain, struggles, heartaches .... you have no memory of people who treated you poorly or situations that happened which created a negative outcome. It's all been washed away.

"The only thing retained from the wash was love and the fruits of love. Every moment of your life where you felt love, comfort and happiness have been retained. All the people you loved have been retained. Every situation you had on Earth that brought a positive outcome has been retained. All these feelings, people and events will be very helpful to you on this side and serve as the foundation that you can build your eternity on.

"Second, please understand that I am the keeper of the book. I am responsible for making sure everyone is here at their appointed time and that your name is permanently fixed into the Book of Eternity. Please do not ask me any questions. All your questions will be answered when you go into the next room. Keep in mind that when you crossed over to this side, time ceased to exist. There is no time on this side, so you have an endless opportunity to ask questions and pursue every possibility you can imagine. But you'll be doing that in the next room, not here, so please hold on to those questions and let me get through this process as quickly as possible so you can begin your hereafter.

"Now when I call your name, you will come up here and get this piece of paper [He holds up a piece of paper that seems to have few words and just a bunch of lines]. You will take this paper and go through this door over here. [He points to a rather simple looking door to his side]. When you go through this door, you will be greeted by your Guardian Angel. Your Guardian Angel has been assigned to you from the very point in your life when you began to formulate your own thoughts, desires and dreams - I think they call it puberty or something like that. Your Angel knows everything about you and will serve you in your eternity as a source and guide in developing your personal eternity. Your Angel will explain every detail of how this side works and the rules of how to develop your eternity.

"So as I call your name, please come up here quickly and get your piece of paper and leave through this door without asking any questions. Trust me; all the answers are on the other side of the door. I am merely here to make sure your name is secured in the Book of Eternity.

"Andrew Damien Smith."

I stand and go up front to pick up my piece of paper.

The man smiles at me, checks my name off in his book and hands me the piece of paper. I look at it bewildered. There's some broken lines at the top and about a third of the way down, it says, 'TODAY I'M GOING TO...' and then the rest of the paper is full of lines. I look up at the man who smiles and motions me to move on so he can call the next name.

As I walk through the door, I am greeted by my Guardian Angel. Wearing a bright white robe, my Angel is smiling broadly and seems full of enthusiasm.

"Hi, Andy, welcome to the hereafter. My name is Christopher, but you can call me Chris if you want."

"My Guardian Angel has a name?" I ask.

"Sure. Remember when you had your confirmation? You had to choose a confirmation name, right? Your confirmation day was the day I was assigned to you, so when you chose Andrew Damien Christopher Smith, I became Chris on this side. Good name, too."

"Does that mean that only Catholics have Guardian Angels with names?"

"Not at all. God gives all the Guardian Angels names, but since the Catholics choose a name at their confirmation, God thought it made sense to let that name stick with your Angel. Personally, God would be delighted if everyone else picked a name for their Angel as well and let Him go about other business, but it really doesn't make that much difference."

I am somewhat amused by this as I begin to look around. We are in what appears to be a huge library, which strikes me as odd, as Chris continues.

"This is the Resource Center. This is the base for your eternity. I have my office here and this will become a place for you to come and visit often."

"It looks like a library to me." I say.

"It is. It has books on everything you can imagine. You can find the answer to any question here. And I know every page of every book. You can ask me any question and I'll be able to tell you exactly where to go find the answer. It's really cool and you'll see how great this place is as you learn more."

We get to another door and Chris opens it. It's a very simple room with a simple table and two large, very comfortable looking chairs on either side. Chris quickly moves to offer me a seat.

"Can I get you something to drink?" he asks.

"Gee, you can drink on this side, huh? Well, what do you have?"

"Anything you want, Andy. That's the nice part of being on this side. The first thing you need to learn is that there are no consequences over here. Remember, everything negative was swept away when you came through the wash. You can eat and drink whatever you like and you will never gain a pound, get heartburn or become drunk on alcohol. Everything on this side is created from the foundation of love in your heart. If you love cheeseburgers, you can eat them all you want and there will never be any consequences. There's no waste on this side. No restrooms, no diet menus, no hospitals, and no rehab facilities. You eat and drink whatever you want because it makes you feel good. No consequences over here," he explains.

Wow, I think, as I'm suddenly thinking this is going to be a very good place to be. Without asking a second time, Chris puts a drink in front of me that doesn't look very familiar. I take a sip and it is delicious. I'm surprised when Chris notices as he is sitting in his chair.

"You need to remember Andy, that I have been with you since you were a teen. I know all your thoughts and have instant recall of your fantasies, desires and tastes. I am your personal library with instant access to every moment of your life. I don't really need to ask you if you want a drink or what you would like."

I'm a little uncomfortable that Chris knows everything about me, but again, Chris sees my concern.

"Also remember that all the bad stuff was washed away when you came over to this side. I still have access to the bad stuff, but only as a reference point to be used when and if needed. But let me explain how all this works and I'm sure you'll begin to understand as we go," he says.

"You get to create your own eternity. It will come from the foundation of love that you brought with you from your life on Earth. It's pretty simple, really. Here's how it works.

"You will go through that door over there and find your room [He points to a simple door on the other side of the room]. The room just has a bed and nightstand because that's where you sleep. When you get up every morning, you take this sheet and decide what you want to do that day. At the top of the page, you list the people you want to see, and then you complete the sentence, TODAY, I'M GOING TO.... and when you are done, you simply go out your door and your day begins.

"There is no time here, so your day can be whatever you would like and last as long as you would like. When you have had enough, you simply come back to your room, go to sleep and when you wake up the next day, it begins with you filling out your sheet again. Pretty cool, huh?"

Chris sees the hesitancy in my eyes and continues.

"Ok. Remember how you often fantasized about sitting on a cloud with Jesus and watching his whole life and asking him questions?"

Wow, he really does know my thoughts.

"That could be one day for you. Simply put Jesus at the top, then complete the sentence: Today, I'm going to sit on a cloud with Jesus where we can watch his life and I can ask him all those questions I've wanted to ask. When you open your door, you'll see Jesus sitting on a cloud ready to answer any questions you have. When you're done and have satisfied that fantasy, you simply go back to your room and go to bed. When you wake up, you can start a new day."

"Wow. Anything I want to do?" I ask.

"Sure. Remember, only love came through the wash. You can't hurt anybody and they can't hurt you. Each day can be whatever you feel like and last as long as you like. For instance, I know your girls were the most important part of your life on Earth. Over here, you can start every day off by going out to breakfast with your girls. Or you can spend a day with each one doing whatever you want. You could write down, Today, I'm going to take my three girls to Disneyworld when they were 6, 8 and 10 years old. You can have their mother go with you if you want. Whatever. And you can set it up any way you want to."

"Wow. So can I go back to Earth and help my girls out through some rough spots?"

"No, you can't interfere with life on Earth. However, that reminds me of another part of the routine that you need to understand. Before you can start your day, you have to check your messages."

"Check my messages?"

"Yes. There will be a box by your piece of paper that has your messages every day. You must check the messages before you fill out your paper because the messages may dictate what you do for the day."

The look of confusion on my face brings a smile to his.

"You see, I know all the other Guardian Angels on this side. We keep in touch and pass along messages any time the situation warrants. Let's say one of your girls is going through a rough spot as you suggested. Her Guardian Angel would contact me and let me know. I would leave a message for you that your daughter is going through some tough times. You can't go back and solve her problems, of course, but you might choose to spend the day with her ... you know, do whatever it was you and her enjoyed doing.... you know how people sometimes will say, gee, I felt real close to my dad today .... I felt as if he was with me ... you know stuff like that?"

I nod, "Yeah, I've heard people say stuff like that."

"There you go ... that's what happens. You see, you may not be able to solve your daughter's problems, but by spending your day with her on this side, you'll serve as a comfort to her on Earth and she'll feel that closeness to you which may help to keep her strong in her tough time. That's why it's really important for you to check your messages every day before you complete your sheet."

"But how will I know if it helped her out?" I ask confused.

"You're always welcome to come here to the Resource Center. I'm always available. I can always get your daughter's Angel to sit with us and explain what's going on. We can see if maybe you need to spend the next day with her as well and come up with ideas of how to spend the day that would best benefit her situation. You always taught your daughters to listen to their hearts and that was excellent advice, my friend. The heart of love is always connected to the other side. As you spend the day with her, you'll know from her heart what her concerns are. And if she's listening to her heart, she'll feel the answers coming from your day with her. That's why it's so important for people to trust their hearts. People who don't listen to their hearts miss out on many good messages coming from people who love them on this side. It's very frustrating as an Angel, I assure you."

I'm starting to understand how this can make a lot of sense to me.... "Are there always messages?"

"Oh no, Andy.... we always screen them and make sure you only get the messages that really need your attention. And it's not always bad stuff. You might get a message from your dad who is on this side asking you to be a part of his day. You can spend a day with anyone on this side by leaving them a message, or if you have a specific fantasy, you can just put it on your paper and go live it."

"Is there any difference?"

"A little. Say you want to meet your dad here at the Resource Center for a cup of coffee and plan out a day together in the future. If you just want to get together and plan a fantasy one on one, you would leave him a message and then you both are able to speak freely. Your sheet gives you the opportunity to fulfill specific fantasies that you have. The fantasies are driven by your heart, so it's your heart that decides what your dad says."

"Cool. So are there any rules to the fantasies you can fulfill?"

He smiles. "No sir, because we washed away all the things that would hurt or disappoint you. Besides, if you think about all the fantasies you had when you were on Earth, for the most part they were pretty positive, nobody got hurt and it was all very enjoyable. That's pretty much what you have here."

Wow. I hesitate as I'm a bit embarrassed to ask but dying to know. Chris smiles again as he knows.

"Yes, there is sex as well. It's a wonderful gift of intimacy that God has given you and over here, nobody ever gets hurt, no hearts are ever broken, and it's always very mutual and exciting."

"Wow. I know some guys who wouldn't have enough time even in eternity to satisfy all their fantasies."

"Well I'm sure there are a lot of men who come with a lot of sexual fantasies, I'll give you that. But you know Andy, once you get into the many possibilities on this side, I think you'll see that sex really isn't that big of a deal here. Remember, you have an eternity. And there really is so much that you can do. Try a little of this and a little of that. It's kind of like an all-you-can-eat buffet. Take something and enjoy it. Have as much as you want. Then try something else. You keep bouncing around to all these wonderful flavors and textures and it's that wonderful variety and knowing that the food will never be gone that makes it so satisfying. Sex can be a part of it, but I'm certain that you will come to realize that it's really not that important with all the other wonderful opportunities you have to create an exciting, fulfilling eternity."

Chris has really got me believing that I truly have gone to Heaven. But I'm not completely sure about all this.

"Does everyone come to this place?" I ask Chris.

"No. You have to have a certain level of love in your heart to come here. Obviously, after we wash away all the negative stuff, we need to be certain that there is enough good pure love in your heart to create a foundation that you can build your eternity on. Heck, if you wash away all the negative stuff in some people, there wouldn't be enough love in their heart to build a thimble on, let alone an eternity of fulfilled fantasies. God has a place for those and all I can tell you is that God is very compassionate and even those people have opportunities to continue to grow and build the love in their hearts with hopes that they, too, will someday be able to go through the wash and have enough love to build their own eternity."

"Cool. But what if you die young?"

"God makes provisions for those who die before they've had the opportunity to build enough love in their hearts. They are well provided for and God certainly takes care of them."

"That's cool." I hesitate in thought before I speak again.

"But what if I run out of things to do? What if I get bored with the whole thing? It is eternity, after all."

"Trust me Andy, you will never get bored here. That's what this Resource Center is for. Remember how you use to love to watch those science shows about the solar system and all the planets? Remember how many times you thought that when you died you hoped that you could go around to all the different planets and check them out?"

"Yeah... hey, I could spend a long day doing that."

"Sure you can, but you can start here at the Resource Center. There are more planets with activities going on than you can imagine. The scientists back on Earth have barely touched the surface of what is going on out in space. In here, we have every planet by name. You can read up on every one of them. You could build a day around each planet, exploring and observing everything about it. And that's just science. There are so many topics and stories in here. Trust me, my friend, you will never run out of anything to do.

"And you might also remember that I have retained every minute of your life. You can always come to me for ideas. Remember how badly you wanted to be a baseball player? What if we took that day you threw your cleats in the trash because you didn't have enough confidence to compete? Why not go back there and try again - this time with all the confidence you need to win. You could build on that for a long time."

"Yeah, but if I made it in baseball, I might not have had my girls."

"Not so on this side, my friend. Remember, it's your fantasy. You create the story and you can make it anything you want it to be. The main thing to remember is that it all comes from your heart, and your heart is full of love and all the fruits of love. You will always have the capacity to create great and wonderful things to do."

Chris has given me so much to think about. I almost don't know where to begin.

"Listen Andy, the best thing to do is just try it. Go lie down and think about it. When you wake up in the morning, pick something simple at first. Write it down on your paper, and go open your door. Maybe start with breakfast with your girls. Come back to your room and take a rest. Maybe next try a nice walk along the beach. As you try a few things, you'll be able to see how it all works and the more you get the hang of it, the more expanded your fantasies will become. And of course, you may wake up and decide to spend a day here in the Resource Center collecting ideas, or talking to me about your life on Earth. I'm always here and you can leave your fantasy at any time and come ask me questions. But if you trust and listen to your heart, I'm sure you'll work things out."

"I suppose you're right. I could ask a million questions, but it might be better to just get out there and do it for a bit."

"There you go. It's like baseball. You can talk strategy all you want, but it's better to just get out there and play the game and pick up the strategies from your experiences. Besides, remember - you can never get hurt. You can never fail. And I'm always here if you run into anything you don't quite understand." With that, Chris leads me to the door that takes me to my room. It's a simple room, but comfortable and warm. I feel a very comforting peace as I walk in. I turn and see Chris smiling.

"Andy, there is so much to learn on this side. I'm certain that I have not told you everything yet. We'll let it evolve naturally. We'll learn as we go. It will all come together, you'll see. I know your heart. It's going to be a great eternity working with you. I'm here if you need anything."

He closes the door as I start my new life as a fantasy fulfiller.

First Day

It took me a while to get to sleep – that's a lot of information to process after all. After sitting on my bed trying to process everything I have heard, I finally lay down to sleep thinking about all Chris had said. I am surprised as I lay down how quickly I fade into a deep and peaceful sleep.

When I wake up the next morning, I decide that my first fantasy would be a simple one. I'm going to just have breakfast with my girls. After that, I'm going to take a walk along the beach and think about other fantasies and maybe put them in order as I stroll along a beautiful beach.

I get up and take my sheet of paper. At the top, I write down, Tracy, Kelly and Rosemary. Then I write; TODAY, I'M GOING TO have breakfast with my girls at a nice, relaxing restaurant.

I put my sheet down and hesitate as I make my way to the door. This is my first time, so I'm obviously a little nervous about how this is going to work. I put my hand on the knob, pause a few moments, then open the door ... only to find myself standing in front of a brick wall!

Frustrated, I try to understand. I did what I'm

supposed to do. It's a simple process, for crying out loud. My fantasy clearly was not to stand there looking at a brick wall!

I storm out the other door and into Chris' office, only to find him relaxed in his chair. He looks up and is smiling as if he knows exactly why I am there.

"My fantasy door is broken! I wanted breakfast with the girls and it gave me a brick wall!" I scream.

Chris stands up and continues to smile as he puts his arm around my shoulders.

"You didn't check your messages, did you Andy?"

The frustration drains out of me as I realize he is right.

"You can't leave the room until you check your messages. It's no big deal, just go back and check the messages."

"But this is my first day. How can there be any messages on the first day?"

Chris smiles at me and says, "Trust me Andy, it's a tradition. Go check your message and have a wonderful day. I'll be here if you need anything."

I'm a bit reluctant, but leave Chris and head back to my room. I go over to the box next to my paper and realize that it is blinking. I'm thinking it's probably some goofy greeting from all the Guardian Angels wishing me luck on my first day. They probably just do that to make sure everyone understands that the messages have to be checked. I push the button that says, Check Messages.

"Andrew Damien, how's me boy doing? Welcome to the other side. Your Mom and I are outside waiting for you. I know you probably wanted to start in on your fantasies, but this is a tradition. Your first day is a family reunion. Your Mom and I will explain it to you when you come out, so come on and let's get this party started. Just write: FAMILY REUNION on your sheet."

I'm frozen. My Mom and Dad are right outside my door waiting for me. Now I'm really nervous. I write down 'FAMILY REUNION' on my sheet and go over to the door again, take a deep breath and slowly open the door.

As I peak around the door, I see Mom and Dad standing there arm and arm with big smiles on their faces. They look great and seem to be in a beautiful park of some sort. I quickly move out the door and into a big hug with my parents. I step back and look at them. They look great. Young - about fortyish or so. They look healthy and happy.

"We're so glad to see you, Andy. We've all been looking forward to this day. You're going to have a great time."

They take my hand and we start to walk towards a beautiful pavilion with a big, full tree hanging tall over it and it appears to be overlooking the ocean. There are a lot of people there mingling about and I ask my Mom who they are.

"It's your family, Andy. Everyone who came here before you. Your Grandparents Granny Dot and Panos, Grandpa and Mary Alice. Hermes, your great Uncle, Ditty, your great Aunt and her husband Chuck, Uncle Carl and Aunt Mimi, Aunt Jean and Aunt Bobbie. Those relatives from your era are here, but after you've had time to visit with them, we are going to take you to another party with all the relatives from the eras before your time."

I'm amazed as my Dad jumps in.

"This is always how you start out on this side. You spend your first day with your family tree. You get to meet everybody and sit and get to know them all. It's a great time. And it will certainly give you plenty of ideas for future fantasies. We've all had some great parties together. It's fun. We get together every now and then over a cup of coffee and decide what the next adventure will be. A bunch of us just got back from a week in Paris. It was the greatest."

I am totally excited as we close in on the party. Grills are smoking with the wonderful aroma of meat grilling, and there seems to be all kinds of food spread out. A bar in the corner with every imaginable beverage you could want. It's a beautiful setting. The perfect setting for reacquainting with those people I loved so much that left my life so many years ago on the other side.

"You all recognize my son, Andrew. This is his first day on this side, so let's celebrate and make him welcome," my Dad announces.

I went to each one and got plenty of hugs. Dad brought me a drink while Mom brought me a plate of food. I was so amazed at the love and the feeling of support for me. Everyone seemed anxious to visit with me. I noticed that everyone seemed to be young. My Dad told me at events like this the age doesn't really matter - you can pick the age you want to be. Everybody usually chooses to be in their prime, obviously. In fact, it seemed like Granny Dot and Panos were the youngest ones there. I brought that to Granny Dot's attention.

"Well, I'm certain that your Grandfather who is always 25 wouldn't want to hang around an 80 year old fuddy-duddy." She laughs as does Panos.

I am amazed at the love I see between the two. Panos died so early. My Mom explains that on this side, you can't choose to be older, just younger, so Panos and Granny Dot are pretty much staying in their mid-twenties. From what I see, my dear beloved Grandmother shows no signs of complaining.

Oddly, my Mom and Dad seem older than their parents, but there is little concern about this. Certainly on this side, age really doesn't matter. We are all just family. You don't get a sense that one is the mother of the other, or that one is the dad of the others. Everyone just seems to be good, close friends with no distinctive structure of family hierarchy.

It is a great feast. I have the opportunity to visit with everyone and there never seems to be any rush. Each relative explains how this side works from their advantage and everyone encourages me to include them in many of my future fantasies - a request I will have no problem obliging.

When I have visited with everyone, my Dad asks me if I'm ready to move on.

"Sure, where are we going?" I say with great enthusiasm.

Hermes points down the beach where in the distance I can see a huge gathering of people.

"That's the rest of your family. Here, you got to see those relatives that you actually knew during your life on

Earth. But those are the family members that came long before your time. You'd be surprised who's in your family tree, Andy. Smiths, Panagiotopulos, Bainbridge, McDoughna, Lungren, Hicks, and so many more families. It's a great family tree and you're going to really get a kick out of meeting all these great people."

With that, we all head for the other party. There is great excitement as we go. Everybody seems to be telling me about the different people I'm about to meet. I can't keep up with all the information, of course, but I certainly get the picture. I'm getting ready for what I am certain will be a celebration of family like I have never imagined.

When we arrive, I look around at literally hundreds of people. You can clearly see the periods from where they came, but again, everyone is young looking and smiles are the norm.

I am introduced by Dad and am quickly handed another drink.

For the next eternity, I am greeted one by one by so many great people. Some of the names I had heard of before and was excited to put a real face to. Others I had never heard of but quickly became close to as they told me their place in my family tree.

I also noticed something that truly excited me. On the other side, I would have been very nervous in this setting, thinking that there was no way I could ever remember all these names and stories being thrown at me. But on this side, everything sticks. Instead of feeling overwhelmed, I am totally enthralled with all the people I am meeting and stories I am hearing. I have this great sense that everything I'm hearing is being retained. This is so exciting because I am quickly realizing that it's a good thing time doesn't matter on this side, as I am coming up with so many ideas for fantasies I want to explore after meeting all these wonderful people. I have so many family members that come from time periods that I always wanted to explore. On this side, not only can I do so, but now I can do so with members of my very own family tree. How exciting is that!

Well this day has totally blown me away. After meeting everyone and hearing all these wonderful stories, I am ready to go back to my room for a rest. It seems like everyone has made me promises to keep in touch and I have promised to include them in some of my future fantasies to be sure.

Wow. I'm exhausted, yet so excited I don't know if I'll ever be able to sleep. When I get to my room, instead of lying down, I head right out the other door to go talk to Chris and share with him all the wonderful stories this day has brought me.

I fly through his door and give him no opportunity to even say hello.

"Unbelievable! You would not believe the day I just had. It was so incredible! I got to visit with my parents, grandparents, aunts, uncles .... wow ... and then they took me to another party where I met members of my family I didn't even know existed! It was something, Chris, and I'm thinking now that I might need an extension on this eternity stuff because I have so many new ideas to explore, eternity may not be enough time."

I stop to get my breath. Chris has the biggest smile.

"Well, we find this is the best way to start. After you leave Earth, there are so many people thinking of you and feeling bad because you have left, we think it's good to send you on a family tree reunion until the emotions on Earth about you being gone are settled and we don't have so many messages to go through. Beside, you've got a great family tree, Andy, and I can tell you won't be coming to me bored and looking for ideas any time soon."

I laugh, recalling how only yesterday I was asking

him that question.

"Yeah. Man, I'm so excited I think I'm going to have to grab one of these books out here to read before I go to sleep."

"Well, you're welcome to grab a book any time, but you also must understand that our pillows on this side are specially designed. As soon as your head hits the pillow, you have no problems going to sleep. But hey, that does remind me of something I need to show you."

Chris gets up and takes me out into the Resource Center and quickly guides me to a wall full of books. He looks at me and smiles.... "You might want to start here."

I look closer at the books. Some of the titles are very familiar. As I gaze from row to row, the confusion on my face forces Chris to explain.

"These are all your stories, Andy. The books and plays you wrote as well as all the ones you never quite got to."

I look at Chris even more confused .... "If I didn't get to them, how did they get done?"

"I wrote them for you. You had a pile of story ideas. You had notes for stories you wanted to develop. You had so many ideas that you could never even get them all written down as ideas. I took every idea and knowing you and how you write, I wrote the stories for you. It's your complete body of work Andy, and I must say it's an impressive collection."

"Every story line I had is here and completed?" I'm dumbfounded.

"Yeap. I know how you develop stories and I was able to complete everything. Go ahead and read one of them and tell me it isn't exactly how you would have written it."

I look back at the collection of books. Wow. So many titles I know instantly where the book titles came from. This is amazing.

"Too bad I couldn't have all this back on Earth."

"Earth isn't that important, Andy. What is important is that it's all here for everyone to experience. The shelf life here is eternity. I think that beats anything back on Earth, don't you think?"

I smile as I select a book that I'm anxious to finally read. Chris sends me back to my room, assuring me that this was just the beginning of many wonderful experiences for me. I am excited. It's been a great day. I have so much to think about. I am spent, and this is only day one of eternity. I lay back on my bed and flip open the book with great anticipation to see how my story line and this book are connected. It's then that I realize that Chris wasn't kidding. These pillows are special. The book will have to wait. I'm fading fast and I'm ready to sleep, knowing that if my first day is any indication of what Heaven is going to be, I'm certainly one lucky person.

God sure knows how to make a Heaven, that's for sure.

Day Two

When I wake up the next day, I sit up in my bed and reflect on the family reunion. I'm thinking I'm going to go back to my first plan and simply have breakfast with my girls. I'm so inspired from yesterday that I just can't wait to see them.

I go over to the stand and check my messages- Nothing there – Good - I grab my pencil and paper and write at the top, TRACY, KELLY AND ROSEMARY. Then I complete the sentence ... TODAY, I'M GOING TO have breakfast with my daughters at a nice restaurant. I go to the door – I'm not nearly as hesitant as yesterday - and open it. There they are - the most beautiful site ever created. They are busy talking as sisters do when they are young adults.

I walk in and am greeted with hugs and kisses as I settle into the booth with them. The muscles in my face are sore from my smile being so large and constant. I'm thinking eternity is going to be great.

As I start on my first cup of coffee, the girls ask me how I'm doing? I start telling them everything about the family reunion yesterday. I'm not missing a detail as my words are flying out faster than I can think them. As I move to the second party that has all the past relatives that I never met, I notice something that brings me to a curious halt. All three of my girls are just sitting there looking at me as if I'm the biggest idiot on Earth. I've seen that look from them before - mostly when they were teenagers and I was trying to give them all my knowledge. This isn't what I was thinking at all for this fantasy.

"Are you guys ok?" I ask.

Rosemary, never the shy one when it came to speaking her mind shoots right back.... "Are you?"

I look all three of them in the eyes and realize that I have lost my girls. In a panic, I excuse myself and run right through my room to the door and into Chris' office. He is shaking his head.

"Hey! My girls think I've gone mad! That's not a fantasy!"

"Andy, sit down. Maybe there are a few more points I need to give you before you really get the hang of this."

He pauses and offers me a drink - setting a cup of coffee in front of me because he's my Guardian Angel and thinks he doesn't have to really ask me.

"I don't want anything to drink, I want to know why

my girls think I'm nuts!"

"Relax Andy, you're doing fine. We just need to go over a few details and you'll have the hang of it in no time. First of all, you have to always remember that when you have a fantasy that involves people who are on the other side - still alive on Earth - you have to have a fantasy that is within their frame of time. If you go out to breakfast with your girls, your fantasy has to stay within their world, not yours. You can create whatever fantasy you want, but it has to be on their side not ours. Any time you talk about this side, your words will be broken Latin and nobody will understand you - and your fantasy will default. It never happened. Is that clear?"

"Well it is now. Seems like that was some pretty good information I could have used beforehand, though. You're not very good at this are you?"

"We're fine, Andy. You'll get the hang of this in no time - because there is no time on this side and only the positive love sticks on this side. It's all good."

I sit back and take a deep breath. Actually, what Chris says makes sense. I take a sip of my coffee and ask him if there is anything else I'm missing?

"Well Andy, let's just review the sheet once again to make sure. Remember now, when you write down the names of people who are still on the other side, you have to become part of the other side. Remember, it's a fantasy, so you can make it what you want, but it has to be within their laws of time. The trip to Disneyworld when they were younger works ... telling them about the family tree reunion yesterday, doesn't work."

I nod now understanding from first hand experience.

"Next, keep in mind that if you write the names of people at the top who are on this side, they will be able to talk with you and participate in your fantasy as you wish them to. Your heart will guide their every word.

"Now you could choose to just be an observer in your fantasy, and in that case you would not put any names at the top of your paper."

I look a bit confused as he continues.

"Let's say you want to go to the Yankee / Cubs game where Babe Ruth made the famous call for the home run."

I perk up – "Oh, that would be so cool."

"OK. If you simply want to see how it really happened, then you would not put any names at the top, you would just write, Today, I'm going to the Cubs / Yankees game to watch the Babe call his famous shot. You will open the door and be able to take a seat in Wrigley field and enjoy the game pitch by pitch. All the fans will be there but none of them will be able to talk to you or see you. You're just observing."

"Now say you want to go out after the game and have a drink with the Babe and talk baseball with him. Well then you would have to write down his name at the top of your paper. You can watch the game and then afterwards head down to the tunnel where the Babe comes walking out, recognizes you and the two of you can go wherever you want, sit and have a couple of beers and talk baseball all night long. Because the Babe is on this side, you can talk to him about baseball up to your day of passing. Everyone on this side understands everything up to the day of your passing. That actually would be a pretty good fantasy if you ask me.

"And finally, if you want to have a non-fantasy meeting with someone on this side you simply put the names of those you want to meet and then write, Today I'm going to meet with my Dad at an outdoor café in a non-fantasy setting so we can make plans for another fantasy. Then your Dad can speak freely because it's not a fantasy that you control. You'd be surprised how many times members of your family get together here at the Resource Center to plan trips. And they really put together a lot of great trips, too. They grab a bunch of books and go through them and wrestle with all the possibilities. Your family sure knows how to have fun."

I smile and nod. "There truly are no dull people in this family tree, that's for sure. So if I want to have a fantasy that involves people from the other side - still living on Earth - I need to keep the fantasy within their time limits and not cross over at any time to this side."

"Right."

"If I want to simply observe something to see how it actually happened but don't need to talk with anyone, I simply write the fantasy description and don't put any names at the top."

"Right again!"

"But if I want to talk with someone - who is over on this side - then I have to put their name at the top, and then complete the sentence."

"Correct again."

"And if I just want to get together with someone and plan a future fantasy, I have to write that it is a non-fantasy setting."

"By George, I think he's got it! And when it rains, where does it rain?"

I look at Chris unimpressed as he howls in laughter, relieved that I'm finally getting how this thing works. Reluctantly, I laugh too, but am anxious to go back and try breakfast again.

I excuse myself and head back to my room. I complete my paper again .... Tracy, Kelly and Rosemary .... Today, I want to have breakfast with my daughters in a nice quiet restaurant. I go over to the door and open it again to find my girls in the same setting. Once again I am greeted with hugs and kisses as I settle into the booth. I am more curious as I begin to make sure there is no sign of what happened earlier. They seem oblivious of my earlier ranting, so I'm thinking Chris got me straightened out ok.

It is a delightful breakfast. For the most part, I do what I always did before when I got together with my girls - I ate my food and pretty much sat back and watched them do all the talking. I always let them dictate the conversation, and given my earlier mishap, I was glad to let them do it now. They looked great and their spirits were so positive. It reminded me how much of Heaven I really had when I was back on the other side. I am so thankful that this side lets me experience this wonderful moment and am certain that I will enjoy this over and over again.

As we finish up, we go our separate ways. I, of course, go back to my room. Instead of resting, though, I want to go ahead and take a nice walk along the beach. I check my messages - nothing there - and grab my pencil ... Today, I'm going to take a nice walk along the sunny beach in the early morning hours. I go and open the door and am stepping out on the beautiful beach. I take a nice long walk. I reflect on so many things. My family reunion and think about all the many possibilities I have to get together with them. I go over the rules again and consider all the different scenarios of fantasies that I might want to explore. But mostly, I just think about my girls. How great is Heaven when I can at any time find myself in the presence of those three girls.

I'm realizing that one of the hard parts about this side is controlling your excitement. I realize that it's important that we all have a room with a bed - and those special pillows to give us rest. I head back to my room and lie down. I'm really enjoying this and am excited to see what tomorrow will bring. As I thank God for my many blessings, I wonder if the girls are going to bed tonight feeling the same closeness to me that I feel for them. I smile as I think that maybe Rosemary is thinking, where did Dad ever learn to speak Latin? I laugh myself to sleep.

Day Three

I wake up and sit up in my bed. I reflect on what I have done so far and think about what I might want to do today. It's not a tough decision, as I already went through my wish list on my walk along the beach. Today, I want to go to my grandfather's office in New York City and see what it was like when he was a big time writer.

I get up and check my messages - nothing – Good - I grab the pencil and write at the top PAUL GERARD SMITH. I pause. Am I sure he's the only one I want to talk to back there? I shake off the thought. This is eternity after all. If I see anyone interesting, I can always hook up with them in a later fantasy. Today, I just want to be with grandpa and see what his world was like when he was the great writer of Vaudeville times. I write... TODAY, I'M GOING TO the W45th St office of Paul Gerard Smith and spend the day talking to him about writing.

I go to the door and open it. I walk into a nice lounge area with lots of chairs and couches scattered in no particular organization. It is clearly 1920 or so. Some of the furniture looks nice and expensive. Some looks like old stuff discarded by others and finding a new home.

As I walk in, I look to my right and see a large rehearsal hall with a piano, stage and big open wooden floor. There is a man playing the piano and a young lady singing next to him. They are working on new material. On the stage are a couple of young men that seem very focused on honing the timing of their routines. Off to the side is another man holding pieces of paper and discussing with another man what seems to be a change he is trying to make to the comic skit he is holding.

There are some people resting in the couches and chairs as I walk by, some talking and some sleeping. Ahead, I see a door wide open with a frosted window and the initials, PGS, stenciled on it. That must be grandpa's office. Typical that he would have his door wide open, as grandpa always welcomed a friend or family member to interrupt whatever he was doing.

I get to the door and peer in. Grandpa is busily typing away, smiling broadly as his fingers fly, throwing letter after letter at the blank piece of paper before him. He looks up and notices that it is me and his fingers come to a screeching halt.

"Hey kid, come on in and make yourself comfortable. What brings you to my world? Can I get you a Dr Pepper?" I laugh, recalling how much grandpa loved his Dr Peppers.

He gets up and comes to me with a big hug. This strikes me as odd. Grandpa wasn't all that warm when I knew him back on Earth. I knew he truly loved his grandchildren, but I don't remember him be outwardly warm as he is now. I guess I didn't know him that well. I always just saw him as the old man. I never spent much time thinking that he might have had a life before he was the old man. But I guess that's the point of this fantasy.

"So this is where you worked, huh?"

"This is it. The hub of Broadway. I have comics, singers and actors coming and going all day long looking for new material or trying to freshen up their old stuff. It's a lot of activity but I love it, kid. To spend your entire day with creative people bouncing ideas off the walls is one hell of a way to make a living. So what would you like to do today?"

"I just wanted to hang out here and see how the master creates his genius."

"Well kid, if a genius ever shows up here, I'll be sure to send you a message."

I laugh. Grandpa was always quick. Quick wit, quick at the typewriter and quick to throw out his opinions.

"Really gramps, I wanted to sit with you and talk to

you about writing. I tried all my life to make it and didn't get very far. I know how hard it is to write really good stuff that nobody wants. I'd love to sit and talk to someone who actually made a living at it."

"Well don't sell yourself short, kid. I've read a lot of your stuff in the Resource Center and I'm telling you if you had been around during this era, you would have a big office like this as well. In this era all you needed was a good story and enough balls to never hear anyone say no to you .... (he smiles sheepishly) …except your grandmother - I always listened to every word Al said to me... I spent a lot of time talking to your buddy Chris and he told me all the stories of you trying to make it back on Earth. I'll tell you something, kid, you got the Smith gene for writing, but you got your mother's patience to be sure. I would have never been able to go as far as you did with all those silly rejections. You're a fine writer Andy, and what happened back there only reflects the notion that the world has forgotten that the job of a writer is to simply tell a good story. Give 'em a good story and let them run with it and you create entertainment. The adventures Chris would tell me about you made me realize you never had a prayer. I guess good stories didn't hold much in your era… it's a shame, really."

He settles into his chair as I grab a chair and move it next to his.

"So when you write a story, gramps, what do you think is the most important ingredient?" I ask him, anxious to get into his writer's mind.

"People. It's all about people. You need to have a main character who is believable, and predictable. You want the audience to fall in love with him right away and know that they will love him throughout the show. Or you want them to hate him right away and know that they will hate him throughout the show. Then you surround him with other characters who create chaos, conflict and controversy. Of course, you need a story or your people just sit there laughing at you on your blank piece of paper with nowhere to go.

"Truth is kid, the most important character in all my stories was your grandmother. Mary Alice was an angel and just thinking of her every day was enough for me. My stories always had to be great because Al deserved nothing but the best." He winks and smiles at me.

This is so exciting. Hearing my own grandfather talking about the craft I loved and tried so hard to master. This is a great treat for me.

We continue to talk writing for what seems like a

flash and yet an eternity. We bounce ideas and stories off one another. I am totally blown away, taking every morsel of conversation and savoring every word my grandfather speaks. I truly am in Heaven and I could easily spend my whole eternity sitting here listening to this creative man tell his stories.

What strikes me as such a pleasant surprise is the mutual admiration we share for each other as writers. Grandpa is quick to ask me my ideas and listens intently to my every response. He laughs a lot ... we both do. I would have thought that there would be a feeling of being way out of my league here ... after all, my grandpa was a great writer during an era where writers ruled the entertainment business. Here I was with my writing resume that was as impressive as Tiny Tim singing with the Mormon Tabernacle Choir. But instead of feeling inferior, we both were equal as we shared all our war stories, embracing our successes and laughing through our failures.

Every question created another. Every response created another story. I could see in his eyes that he was enjoying this as much as I was. I never looked at my grandfather like I did today. What a truly remarkable man. What a wonderfully creative mind. And what a truly loving and passionate man. This is the man I simply looked at as the old man for many years while we were on Earth. I see now how much I missed with that earthly vision, and I embrace this world of eternity where the opportunity comes to correct such shallow visions.

But we get to a point where we need to stop. I'm certain that he is anxious to get back to his loving wife and family. I am satisfied, knowing that on this side, there will always be opportunities to come back. Many more fantasies to explore with grandpa.

I thank grandpa for this incredible day and we promise each other that this was not the final visit. A warm hug from a man I have gained so much respect for... a man who has shown that he is so much more than an old man... a man that I am so thankful passed his wonderful genes my way.

As I'm walking out his door, grandpa stops me.

"Hey kid, the library has a lot of your work and you will have lots of opportunities to realize what a great writer you really were. I've read everything – and I'm privileged to know that my genes as a writer were passed along to such a creative mind. Don't think for a minute you're second class, kid." He winks again and smiles.

As I enter my room, I am once again too wound up to

think about sleeping. I don't have to think much though; I know all too well what the best medicine for me is. I go to the desk and see that there are no messages and then I take the pencil and write ... TODAY, I'M GOING TO take a nice walk along the beach at the break of dawn. I go to my door and step outside. This time a different beach, but still the great, wonderful tranquilizer my rushing soul needs after spending the day with grandpa.

It's a great walk. A calming walk that seems to help me sort everything out.... the day with grandpa and his wonderful compliments to me as a writer can not be put into words. I had so much rejection as a writer on Earth, yet today the greatest writer I have ever known told me he loved my stories. How could I ever think about sleeping again?

As I head back to my room, I realize that a walk along the beach will likely become my personal bedtime story every night. I am refreshed and comforted. I am at peace with everything going on. I am ready to rest and excited in knowing that tomorrow starts another day. I thank God for letting me have this opportunity to see my grandfather in such a wonderful setting. I am spent, but I'm also completely satisfied as my heart is flowing in love and gratitude for the day given me.

I am thinking that my prayers on this side will be an enthusiastic redundancy of two words ... Thank You ... it's the only thing I can come up with ..... thank you .... thank you.... thank you .... if that's all you have to say when you pray to God, then you must be in Heaven.

Day Four

When I wake up in the morning, I sit up thinking those pillows sure are great. It's hard to get use to the idea that time doesn't mean anything on this side, but I sure am beginning to understand that when I lay my head on those pillows, I am going to get a deep, peaceful sleep unlike any I ever had in my life on Earth. I feel great and refreshed.

I sit on the side on my bed thinking how I might want to start my day off. I know what I want to do today, but I'm also starting to get the hang of this place and feeling like I might want to try a few things out.... maybe I should start with breakfast down by the beach with the girls? .... maybe I could start the day with a nice baseball game .... maybe I could give this sex thing a try - no, I'm not comfortable with that one .... I know Chris is my Angel and is looking out for me, but sex with anyone I want? Sounds like a set up to me ... it's an awful selfish way to spend time here, even if it is ok..... you know, I think it would be great to have breakfast down by the beach with Jesus. Informal. I'd like to talk to him about some of the things in the bible and get his take on it.... we could have a nice relaxing chat ... and maybe I'll slip in a question about the sex thing to see if Chris was square with me or if it's just a set up..... Yeah, I'm thinking that would be cool.

I get up excited but also a little hesitant ... after all, I'm going to ask for breakfast at the beach with the Savior of all mankind.... seems a little rude or imposing, I suppose, but I really would love to talk with him and I really don't have any hidden agenda .... well, maybe I should just drop the sex issue altogether - that would be rude ... ask the Savior of all mankind if it's really ok if I have sex with anyone up here and I might find myself flying through the wash and getting all the negative gunk back in my heart..... Yeah, I think sex is a dead issue for at least the first thousand years I'm here.

I go over to the desk and the message machine is blinking – I've got a message ....hey, maybe it's grandpa wanting me to hook up with him today ... cool .... I push the Check Messages and it's Chris.

Hey Andy, your daughter Rosemary is going through a little rough spot right now ... you might want to spend some time with her today.

I panic ... oh no, not my Rosemary ... I fly through the door that leads to Chris' office and nearly dive into his lap ...

"What's wrong with Rosemary? ... What's happened

to her? ... What can I do to make things right for her?"

Chris looks like he just walked into a hurricane - and I suppose he did.

"Whoa.... whoa.... whoa ... hold on there, Andy. Let's sit down and relax, already."

"Relax?! You leave a message saying my girl is going through a rough time and ... what ... you expect me to casually strut in here and say, hey, dude angel, what's happening?"

Chris is sitting back in his chair. He looks as if he has no intentions to respond to me. He's just smiling and staring at me!

"Well?! .... You know they may have washed away all the negative stuff when I came here, buster, but don't test me on my girls, 'cause I can regenerate a whole lot of negative in a heartbeat....." my face is boiling red by now.

Chris shakes his head, smiling.

"Well Andy, your heart is certainly in the right place, I'll give you that. But I'm not going to respond to you until you are relaxed enough to listen to what I have to say, because you are not going to like what I have to say."

I blow up again.

"What!?! Is she hurt bad? ... What happened?

...Whatever the bad news is I can handle it, but you simply can't tell me I have to sit down and 'R-E-L-A-X' when you tell me stuff like this."

"Andy, PLEASE sit down. When I say you're not going to like what I have to say, I'm not talking about Rosemary, I'm talking about you."

"What do you mean you're talking about me? You leave me a message saying that I need to spend the day with Rosemary because she's going through a tough time and all I'm doing is asking you what the hell's going on so I can go back there and plan my day in a way that will help her out the best. Now what is so wrong about that?"

"Well there's nothing wrong with that, really, but the problem is that I can't tell you what's going on with Rosemary until after you spend the day with her."

"Who came up with that rule? I mean what good will it do AFTER I spend the day with her?"

"It will be perfect because then it will only serve to validate the pure love in your heart for Rosemary and hers for you," he says annoyingly calm.

I'm confused, but I have a feeling I better sit down and just shut up before I get myself in trouble, as Chris continues.

"Remember when I talked to you about listening to your hearts? Remember how I complimented you on teaching your girls to listen to their hearts? Remember how I said that hearts of love are always connected? I want you to go back in your room and think about Rosemary. I want you to think of how you want to spend the day with Rosemary. I want you to be still and listen to your heart. Relax and trust your heart. Your heart will never lead you in the wrong direction. I promise you Andy, if you listen and follow your heart, you are going to be able to do so much more than if you come running in here screaming every time you're not sure about something."

He pauses as I take in what he has said. This is harder than I thought. He makes sense, of course, but my concern for Rosemary, without knowing what my concern is for, is really tough. I get up conceding and start for the door. Chris stops me.

"Andy, trust your heart. You have a great heart. That's how you got through the wash. Trust Rosemary's heart. You've raised her to be a wonderful woman with a strong and passionate heart. Let your hearts have this day. And PLEASE, don't THINK. Don't get together with her and ask her a bunch of questions about what's going on - remember, she doesn't understand Latin."

I smile and shake my head.

"This isn't going to be easy you know. I mean can't you even give me an idea?"

"Andy, trust your hearts. In fact, I'm willing to bet that when you come back here after your day with Rosemary, you're going to be able to tell me what she's going through without me telling you ... but only if you listen and trust your hearts."

I take a deep breath and start out the door, when Chris stops me again.

"Oh, and by the way Andy, the idea of having breakfast at the beach with Jesus is not rude or imposing at all. He'd be delighted."

I smile and am flushed with warmth as I turn and head for my room to consider what my next day will be.

I sit and start to think of Rosemary and as I do, I start to get excited. I get to spend an entire day with Rosemary... Wow.... I could spend a whole day in the middle of a traffic jam with Rosemary and it would be a great day. But I have to think of Rosemary.... what would she like to do ... I remember the day I spent with her walking around Balboa Park when we all went back to San Diego. That was one of my favorite days ever.... you know, Rosemary loves animals so much, I'm thinking maybe we should hook up at the San Diego Zoo and spend the day walking around there. She would certainly love that. ... but how do I know that's what she needs? ... ok, I'm thinking again ... I know she will love the day at the zoo and I just need to go with that...

I get up and go to write on my paper when I notice the message machine is blinking again. What's that all about? ... I reluctantly press Check Messages and it's Chris.

Andy, the San Diego Zoo came from your heart... you're on track, my friend ... have a great day and remember to let her start the conversations ... I'll see you after your day.

I quickly write down Rosemary's name and then ... TODAY, I'M GOING TO spend the day walking around the San Diego Zoo with my favorite Brunette, Rosemary!

I move to the door and am anxious to open it and see Rosemary. I throw the door open and there she is, standing in front of a pond with a bunch of pink Flamingos walking about behind her. The smile on Rosemary's face melts me as I quickly move to her and we embrace in a nice, long, warm hug.

We catch up for a bit - me desperately trying to avoid Latin and seeing that pained look on her face. Chris was right, though. By letting Rosemary start the conversations, I am better able to avoid any stupid mishaps like the first day we had breakfast. Rosemary is setting the pace and she sounds so excited. We get a map and plan out our entire day. And oh what a day it was.

Rosemary is my number three daughter. There were so few times I really got to be alone with her. This day really is a treat. I can tell it's a treat for her as well. We talk a lot. Actually, she talks a lot and I just respond to what she says. We stop and study every animal the zoo has and it is so clear to me that I definitely made the right choice today. We laugh a lot, tell stories and embrace every moment of the day. This is when I am so thankful that time has no impact on this side. I am in no hurry to see this day end, and I can sense that Rosemary is willing to test the rules of eternity as well.

But we finally end up at the pond with the Flamingos, having visited every animal and explored every corner of this wonderful zoo. It's time to say goodbye for now. We embrace each other in a long, warm hug that makes me almost feel as if we will squeeze each other into one being. I promise her many more days like this and I encourage her to keep following her heart. I thank her for being such a wonderful person and tell her how proud I am to be her dad.

We hug again and I turn to go back to my room. Of course, I bolt through my room and into Chris' office where he is waiting for me with his usual smile.

"Well, how's Rosemary? Is she ok? Do I need to spend another day with her? What's going on?"

"Andy, sit down ... relax .. She's fine. Now remember, I bet that you could tell me after your day with her, so you tell me."

I stare at Chris in thought ..... zoo .... animals ..... I got it!

"She got bit by a dog! Is she ok? Did she have to get shots? Tell me everything!"

Chris bursts out in laughter as I sit back a bit embarrassed and confused. I thought that was a pretty good guess but apparently not based on the laughter at the other side of the table. Why, my Guardian Angel is practically in tears.

"No, Rosemary did not get bitten by a dog. She had to have a tooth pulled."

I sit back with pained confusion wrapped all over my face.

"WHAT!?!" I exclaim.

"Yeah, she had a tooth pulled and she was kinda

worried about it."

We stare at each other desperately trying to sort this all out.

"So, tell me this Chris ... if she's in a wreck and is bleeding profusely from several parts of her body, what EXACTLY kind of day am I suppose to have then?!"

Chris shudders in horror ... "Andy really, you shouldn't think like that on this side."

"Hey pal, I'm just asking .... I mean Rosemary's a pretty tough cookie and I'm thinking her getting a tooth pulled would not exactly send her through a whirlwind of anxiety, here. It just seems like you're making a bit much out of one tooth, that's all I'm saying."

"Well that's true Andy, but you also have to remember that she is self employed. She works hard and is doing well trying to build her business and make ends meet. Now you know that Rosemary wasn't the best at handling financial struggles. She's not bad, but it's really not one of her strengths. It wasn't about the tooth, it was about her worrying about having to struggle because she had to have this added expense."

I sit back and consider what Chris has told me.

"You know Andy, if you remember the conversations

you had during your day at the zoo"

I interrupt.... "Hey, you know, come to think of it, she did ask a lot of questions about the times when I struggled and how I handled it. Wow ... it all makes sense now."

"Exactly ... that's what I'm saying about listening to your hearts. You know, while you were walking around the zoo, she was under the gas at the dentists office and when she was, we were able to connect your day at the zoo with her heart and she was able to dream about it while you lived it in your fantasy."

"Really ... how cool is that ... the whole thing?"

"Yep. Next time you have a fantasy with her, it wouldn't surprise me if she tells you about the dream she had while she was getting her tooth pulled .... of course, it wouldn't surprise me either that you would jump right in and try to explain how the dream was all part of your fantasy in Heaven and ... well... you know .... the Latin ...."

"You're going to throw that at me every time aren't you?"

"Hey, this is eternity ... I can ride that pony for a long time." He says smiling broadly.

We both laugh. I understand more with each day, and it all makes sense to me. I'm ready to rest. But Chris isn't quite done with me.

"By the way, I see that you're thinking I'm just testing you about the issue of sex?"

Boy, he's starting to scare me. He knows way too much.

"Well I don't know about all that. I mean it kind of makes sense I suppose, but really, it seems like a real selfish act for me. Having sex any time I want with any woman I want ... it just seems to degrade what it's all about. Don't get me wrong, sex is great and it has been a long time. But I look at Mom and Dad ... I watched Granny Dot and Panos ... Grandpa and Mary Alice ... I can see the love there and understand how sex would be a great part on this side. But randomly having sex with whomever I want doesn't seem right. I'm thinking it has to be special and that to be special, it has to be with that one and only true love of your life."

Chris smiles, "Your heart serves you well, Andy. You know, that's one fantasy you've been avoiding."

I look at him, knowing exactly what he's saying, as I start to get up from my chair.

"Yeah, well, you're the one who said that the heartaches get washed away when you come to this side. I'm guessing that's a piece of Heaven I'll just have to do without." I head out the door into my room.

"Remember Andy, this is Heaven. Listen to your heart and let your Heaven come to you."

I turn to Chris and smile.

"Well, you just let me know how Rosemary's tooth turned out, ok?"

Chris smiles and nods as I close the door and lay down on my bed.

It's been an incredible day. I've learned a lot and being with Rosemary today was absolute Heaven. I know that I will not wait for another message to spend the day with her. And certainly, Tracy and Kelly will also get their days. I think about that breakfast at the beach with Jesus and how Chris says Jesus would be 'delighted.' Tomorrow, I'm starting my day with that.

And as I begin to fade, I think about what Chris said. That piece of Heaven that I'm avoiding. I'm wondering if my heart will ever be strong enough to approach that part of Heaven. I hope so, but I know that it will take a long time before I can trust that I can have that fantasy and only feel the love that I know is there .... a love without any consequences. That would be my very best Heaven.

Day Five

When I get up, I know immediately how my day is going to start - given there are no messages, of course. I get up and see that there are no messages - good - I write down Jesus and then ... Today, I'm going to have breakfast with Jesus Christ at a quiet beachfront resort.

I go to the door and open it to find exactly what I was hoping for. A beautiful sunrise coming out of the ocean and there is Jesus sitting at a table taking it all in. I step out and move towards him and he smiles as he sees me coming. Suddenly I stop. It hits me that I am walking towards Jesus, the Savior of all mankind! The man who went through so much pain for me. The man who healed and made so many whole again in their hearts. I am suddenly overwhelmed and feeling that I have no right to be here with this great man.

Jesus understands and gets up to come to me. I am certain that the expression on my face leaves no doubt about the fear and anxiety in my heart.

"Andy, I'm glad you came. I've been looking forward to this day for a long time."

I'm a bit uncertain.... "You have?"

"Of course. Speaking to the multitudes never did much for me. I much prefer these one on ones."

I hesitate, but he guides me to my chair and we sit down to a wonderful table full of food and drink. I notice that Jesus likes his eggs sunny side up, which strikes me as oddly obvious. I still don't know where to begin or how to talk to Jesus, the Savior of all mankind. It's a bit awkward, to say the least. Jesus understands this and is quick to make me feel comfortable. He really knows how to help me relax and loosen up. I guess when you're the Savior of all mankind, figuring out stuff like this must be pretty easy.

By my second mimosa - Jesus does great wine drinks, that's for sure - I was beginning to be more comfortable and started asking Jesus those questions I had been hoping I could. I was amazed at how open and freely Jesus answered my questions. There was no sense of anything being off limits with him. Of course, I was so moved by his passion and enthusiasm as he spoke. I thought there would be a lot of disappointment in how we humans have screwed so many things up back on Earth, but he was just the opposite. He spoke with a lot of encouragement and optimism.

I ask him about times I've let him down or missed opportunities to do the right thing. Or all those times when my thoughts were less than pure.

He smiles, "Andy, those things don't come through the wash. You have to understand that the wash is the crucifixion. All the negative dies there. Only the good comes to this side."

He picks up a rather thick book and hands it to me.

"Andy, this is your life book that Chris and I reviewed before you came through the wash. Now, I don't really need the book, but it might help you to understand the impact you had in your life that you may have never realized. Your PIP number is really quite impressive."

I look at the book, then at Jesus, "My PIP number?"

"Yes, your Positive Impact on People number. In this book are all the people you had a positive impact on. The first section is full of people whom you said something nice to or made a nice gesture … a simple act that simply made them feel better at the time. There are a lot of people in that section. Then in section two are the people that you actually had a part in turning their life into a positive direction. Maybe it was something you said, or something you wrote that really impressed them. What you said or wrote added to what others were saying or writing that helped to turn a negative life into a positive direction. You have an impressive number of people in this section."

I open the book and start to recognize names in my life, before I look up at Jesus who is smiling at me.

"But the third section is the best. There are only forty seven people in it, but these are the people you had a profound impact on. Your daughters, of course are there, but there are some really good stories in this section." He pauses before he continues, "Remember that story you always told people about the girl you ran into at the strip club when you were delivering food?"

My eyebrows rise in horror.

"You always tell that story as a joke, but do you realize that was one of your greatest moments?"

My blank look answers Jesus who smiles at me.

"You tell people how hard it was for you to keep your eyes at eye level when she was talking to you – she was a very attractive young lady – but what you don't know is how hard it was for her to even approach you. She recognized you right away when you came in and she wanted to come say hello… but she was afraid that you would be disappointed in her for working there… but you made such an impact in her youth when she was in that psych hospital that she took the chance …. And you kept your eyes at eye level and treated her kindly without judging her."

I have no response but am numb to what Jesus is saying.

"You know Andy, she left work early that night and after she tucked her child in at bedtime, she sat in her bedroom and cried like she had never cried before. Then she prayed to me saying if Andy believes in me and doesn't judge me, I can believe in myself and stop judging myself."

The tears are falling over the edge of my eyes. I never imagined I had any such impact.

"She quit being a stripper the next day, signed up to go back to school and do you know, Andy, she is one of my best people down there right now… a great mother and wife … and one of the most positive people going. She's done so well because you kept your eyes at eye level."

I sit back bewildered. This is way more than I ever imagined.

"There are forty seven other stories like that in there Andy. If you ever question your being here, I want you to open this book to the third section and read some of these wonderful stories that are there because of you."

I am humbled. "I had no idea I had such an influence on anyone outside of my daughters."

Jesus smiles, "Are you kidding? You had great impact on many people. You really should spend some time looking through this book that your life has created. It's very impressive."

I thumb through the book a little before asking Jesus what my PIP number was and how do they get it?

"Well, you know how people down there love their formulas and statistics... of course, I don't need the formula – I know your number by simply looking at your heart ... but we start with your social number – it's the number between 1 and 10 that reflects the opportunity you had to make an impact on people. The Pope ... Presidents ... people like that have a social number of 1 or 2 ... people with a 10 social number had little or no opportunity to have an influence on anyone. You were a social ranking of 7 .... You didn't have a lot outside of your family and friends."

I hang my head a little, "Yea, I sure didn't make a name for myself, did I?"

Jesus smiles, "Oh, that doesn't matter, Andy ... you gave the writing thing a shot and it never took off ... that's not your fault – I loved your writing."

I look up and Jesus is smiling at me.

"So, then we look at your book. The people in section

one count one point each… the people in section two count as two and the people in section three count as three… we add them up and multiply them by your social number and that gives us your Pip number. You had a PIP number of 152,992, which is a whole lot of positive impact in one's life if you ask me."

I look at Jesus unsure of what to make of the number.

"Numbers are not the important thing, Andy … the important thing is to read these stories and understand the tremendous impact your life had on others. You really did a great job down there. We gave you one life and in return, you gave us forty seven wonderful, positive lives. No matter how you look at it, that's a pretty good return on our investment, don't you think?"

"How's my number compared to others?"

Jesus laughs, "I don't compare, Andy. Your life was not in competition with anyone else's life. I don't really care about the numbers – it's just a formula Chris and the Angels use because they get into that sort of thing … the Guardian Angels are quite competitive, if you ask me. To me it's all about heart – and your heart served you so well."

I take some of my mimosa as I consider all that Jesus

has shared with me. I know I'm going to spend a lot of time looking through this book, that's for sure.

We talked about other topics ... those questions I have always wanted to ask. The more he talked the more questions I wanted to ask. We covered so many topics and Jesus never seemed rushed or in any hurry to wrap this up. He even gave me some pointers on some of my future fantasy plans. It was an incredible morning.

I get to a point where I feel the need to wrap this morning up. After all, he is Jesus, the Savior of all mankind and I really don't want to hog him all to myself for too long - even though he doesn't seem to mind. I don't know what to say to him except thank you. I thank him for everything and especially meeting me like this to talk to me. He is so warm and kind. He really makes me feel as if he would not have chosen any other way to start a day than this. He of course encourages me and tells me how well I'm adjusting to the new world.

He gives me a hug and I head back to my room. I sit on my bed. I am humbled at the experience but also completely satisfied. I'm not sure what else I should do today. I'm thinking it might be good to spend some time in the Resource Center and browse around. Jesus gave me some cool tips on some planets to look up that I might enjoy. That might be the best way to spend my day after a breakfast with the Savior of all mankind, after all.

It's then that I notice that my message light is blinking again. If Rosemary has to have another tooth pulled, I'm going to have to go against the rules and kill Chris.

Hey Andy, this is your Dad. Your Mom and I have a surprise for you. Just write down Today, I'm going to spend the day with Mom and Dad. Hurry up, we're waiting outside.

I do as I'm told and head for the door. I open it and there's Mom and Dad, dressed fancy and looking great! They are standing outside a large building - very artsy looking.

"Come on son, you're going to enjoy this one."

I head with them into the building and it appears to be a big concert hall. High ceilings, very eloquent and all the people seem very excited and anxious to go in and find their seats.

"Come on, we have our seats up in the balcony," my Dad seems so excited.

We climb the stairs and Dad opens the door leading into the concert hall. I am greeted by many familiar faces.

"We invited everyone in the family to join us and we filled up the entire balcony."

I make my way to my seat through many hugs, waves and greetings. So many of my family tree are here. This is great.

"So who are we going to see?" I ask Dad.

"Everybody who's anybody is performing tonight. Your Grandpa, Uncle Hermes and I put this show together and we thought you might enjoy it."

The lights go out and everyone settles into a quiet anticipation. Suddenly, the music crashes into a very familiar run. I know that crashing start by heart - I should because I wrote it! I look over at Dad who is smiling from ear to ear. I look back to the stage and the spot comes up on Billy Joel who starts singing *I'll Keep The Coffee Warm Tonight* exactly the way I heard it so many times in my head - if not better.

Dad leans over..... "Your Grandpa, Hermes and I went over every one of your songs and matched each song with the perfect performer. Tonight, we're going to hear The songs of Andy Smith - done the way they were meant to be done."

I am speechless. I look around the balcony and see my family tree enjoying my songs. I look down on the floor of the hall and there are people everywhere, moving to the beats of my music.

What a surprise, indeed. One by one, the greatest

performers to ever play come on and perform another familiar song of mine. It is such a treat to hear my songs the way I always heard them in my mind. Anyone who has ever tried to be a songwriter knows exactly what this night is all about. It has nothing to do with fame and fortune. It's all about hearing your songs performed with passion by people who get what you are saying and seeing the people listening to it embrace it and appreciate the creative talents that brought it to the stage that evening.

An incredible evening. After the show, the family tree went across the street and we all took over a nice bar there. I made the rounds, talking to everyone and hearing all the people in my family telling me how much they enjoyed this evening.

One by one, the family started to empty the bar and head back to wherever they came from. Finally, it was me, Hermes, Mom, Dad and Grandpa sitting at a table.

"You know kid, there's more where that came from. The three of us are already working on one of those plays you wrote.... Grandpa turns to Hermes .... where did you want to put that one on?"

"London ... they have a grand theater there that would be just great."

"Yeah, that's right ... your Dad is coordinating everything so it should be another great evening."

"Maybe we could all work on some of your plays?" ... I toss out to Grandpa.

"Sure, kid. We have eternity after all. It will be fun for all of us to work together"... he pauses, takes a sip from his drink and smiles ... "You know, our family will certainly be well entertained with us over on this side, but I can't help but think... what the hell do people do for eternity when their family tree is full of plumbers?"

We all nearly fall out of our chairs in laughter. His point is well taken, though.

It's been a great evening, but it's time to rest. I say goodbye to Mom, Dad, Grandpa and Hermes and head back to my room.

I am stopped by Hermes ... "Hey, Andy. Your Mom, Dad, Granny Dot, Panos, Ditty, Chuck and I are planning a trip to the Panagiotopulos estate in Greece. You want us to include you?"

I turn to Hermes .... "You better. I would love to see that."

With that, I'm back in my room. I decide to go into the Resource Center to relax and maybe check a few things out. Chris is already sitting at one of the tables reading through a few books.

"Hey Andy. How did your day go?"

I told him everything. Breakfast with Jesus... the concert with all my songs ... the enjoyable time in the bar with the family tree.

"You know Chris, Grandpa made a comment that we all laughed at but I'm just wondering .... What DO people do when their family tree is full of plumbers?"

Chris laughs.... "Well, you don't bring your JOB over to this side, Andy, you bring your passion. Your passion is creative writing and it just happens to be the passion of many in your family. Some people have a real passion for camping or exploring the wilderness. Some have a passion for many other things. Your passions are passed on from generation to generation. That's by design so that when you come through the wash, your family has similar passions to work with."

It certainly makes sense to me. I'm really happy that my family has so much passion for entertainment. We can fill a lot of eternity with some pretty cool shows, I'm thinking.

After talking with Chris, I realize that I really am kind of beat. Instead of doing any research tonight, I'm thinking I'll just head back to my room and rest. It's been a long day, but a truly wonderful day.

"Listen Chris, I was thinking I might start my day tomorrow here in the Resource Center. Jesus gave me some names of some planets that I might find interesting and I thought I might check them out and plan out my day from that."

"Sounds good Andy. I know right where to go and I think you'll be surprised at what you can find. You did well today. You seem to be getting a hang of this side pretty well."

"Yeah, I'm getting more comfortable with it. I think you just have to realize that time doesn't apply on this side. I'm slowly learning to take my time with these fantasies and let them really develop and go their course without being anxious to move to another one."

"It's the hardest thing to adjust to on this side," says Chris in agreement.

"Oh hey, Chris.... How did Rosemary's tooth episode work out?"

"Great! Your day with her at the zoo really helped her out. She went home from the dentists and decided that she was going to stop worrying about finances. She realizes that happiness comes from relationships and not bank accounts."

"That's my girl!... How are the others doing?"

"They're fine. They miss you but then you're such a miss-able kinda guy you know."

I smile.

"I miss them, too." ... but for now, I'm going to catch some rest. It's been a great day.

With that, I get back to my bed and lay down. I think about breakfast with Jesus, the Savior of all mankind, my PIP number, the concert with my family and how my songs really came to life. I am so appreciative of my family and the love I continue to feel with every experience on this side.

I'm starting to think Heaven is going to be a pretty nice way to spend eternity.

Day Six

I wake up to day six. I have had some wonderful experiences and can see that with every experience, I am coming up with so many more ideas of how to spend a day here in eternity.

But today I'm thinking I want to start out in the Resource Center. I'm thinking it would be nice to walk around and really see what that place is all about to help me better in the future.

I check my messages and there are none, so I go out the door that leads to the Resource Center and see Chris sitting at one of the tables browsing through a book. He probably knows what I was going to do before I did and that's starting to annoy me a bit - even though annoyance supposedly didn't come through the wash, but Guardian Angels sure can challenge that notion.

Chris notices me.... "Hey Andy, how you doing today?"

"Well Chris, I thought I'd spend the day here in the Resource Center to get familiar with it and maybe check out a few places Jesus told me about."

"Good idea. Sit down and let me give you an overview and then I can show you around."

I sit down reluctantly as I am learning that arguing with Chris is not going to get me anywhere - even though I was kind of looking forward to browsing and discovering this place alone. But maybe an overview might be good.

"First, this Resource Center is your families Resource Center. Every family tree has their own Resource Center. It's especially designed for your family, utilizing all the interests and passions that are inherent in your family history. From generation to generation, your Resource Center has been growing. Every time a member of your family comes through the wash, this Resource Center grows up to the date of your passing."

I look a bit confused.

"Ok, you remember how I told you that your grandfather, Panos, could not go beyond his day of passing at 25 years?"

I nod - now even more confused. "Yeah."

"What I meant was that he could not create any fantasy that would have him older than 25 years because there is no reality that registers him beyond his 25th year. He will always have fantasies within the 25 years of reality registered.

"However, every time a family member passes through the wash, that day becomes the new 'up to' day from which fantasies can occur for any member of your family tree. That's one reason why everyone is so happy to see you. They now have a whole new block of time that they can explore and develop their fantasies from."

"So you're saying Panos - because I'm here - can now go to New York City in the year 2032, but he has to be 25 years old or younger?"

"Exactly! All the books here at the Resource Center became updated to 2032 on the day you came through the wash, not to mention all the new additions of your personal writings that were added on that day as well. And as you learned on your first day, you retain everything on this side because it all comes from love. So while you were getting indoctrinated with me, all your family members were here in the Resource Center getting all the updates."

"But I came through here and I didn't see anybody. In fact, every time I come here the place is empty."

"That's right. The Resource Center is a place for you to come and research whatever you want. You must be able to do so without a lot of distractions. So every time you come here, it will be empty - unless it's written on your paper that you want a non-fantasy day at the Resource Center with whomever's name you put at the top of the paper."

"So Panos, who came here in the early 1920s, now can completely understand how computers work and how people can get from Paris to New York in a matter of hours?"

"Absolutely. But it comes gradually. Your family members who lived during the time of Jesus now understand how computers work too, but they have been gradually learning how all these things have evolved as every passing generation has come through the wash. It's never overwhelming and actually becomes an exciting way to spend a day. This Resource Center really gets a lot of use - especially when a new family member comes through the wash."

I'm fascinated by all this but as I think about it, it makes a lot of sense. I'm not inclined to challenge any of this with more questions because I'd rather get up and start exploring this place on my own. I start to get up.

"Well thanks Chris that really helps out. I think I'll just browse around and kind of get a feel for this place for a bit."

"Ok, I'll leave you be," says Chris, "but before I do, let me point out a few things".... he gets up and stands by me

.... "As you can see, the topic is clearly marked ... over there is science ... there's history ... over there is music .... you can figure that out I'm sure.... now in front of every section, there is a stand that just has a flat square on it ... do you see it over there at the science section?"

I look closer and sure enough there is a stand that looks somewhat like a music stand but is just flat and inconspicuous... "Yeah, I see it."

"They have one of those at every topic. They are called the Finders. They are connected to everything in that topic. Now, let's say you want to look up those planets Jesus was telling you about ...."

I nod enthusiastically ...

"You would put one hand over your heart and the other hand on the Finder and the desire of your heart would connect with the Finder and the best book for you would automatically start blinking so you can find it."

"Get outta here .... That's all I have to do? How cool is that. That's way better than having to figure out all the codes on a library card, I'm telling ya."

"It is nice, but be careful. You really need to be specific before you connect your heart to the Finder. In this case you would concentrate ... I want to check out the planets that Jesus was telling me about ....concentrate .... your hand on your heart ... the other on the Finder ... bingo ... the book you need is blinking until you get it. Or, you can ask a question .... I'd like to check out the best planets to go surfing ... hand over your heart ... other on the Finder ... there it is ... the best planets to go surfing blinking away."

"Wow, this is going to be fun," I pause "But why did you say to be careful? There's more to it, right?"

"Well, you have to be concentrating on what you want to find before you put your hand on the Finder. If you start to wander away from what you're looking for as you put your hand on the Finder, it will be confused and smack you."

"Smack me?"

"Oh, yes... and it's a most unpleasant experience, I assure. If the information is unclear, the Finder sends it back to you with a nasty dose of current to smack you back into concentrating. It usually happens when a few people are here planning future fantasies. One will cover their heart and then start talking to the other as they put their other hand on the Finder ... Smack! .... Boy, those people jump when that happens ... but in most cases, it only happens to a person once before they learn to stay focused when standing near the Finders.

"Now over here is where I showed you all your books, plays and scripts, remember?"

"Yeah ... I definitely want to spend some time in that area."

"You sure do, because I didn't tell you everything ... that's your family room. All your Grandfather's works, Carlton Smith ... it is filled with your relative's writing ... there's even a section of your Dad's scripts."

"Dad's scripts?"

"Sure. Your Dad always wanted to write scripts for movies. Don't you remember all those times you talked to him and he was giving you ideas for stories? Your dad had a most creative mind and even though it never materialized back on Earth, those ideas became scripts over here and are yours to enjoy."

"How cool is that! I always thought he should have been a writer. Alright, Pops!"

"And here's the nice thing, Andy. You can get one of your Dad's script... read through it, and if you want, just go over to that door over there and step in - and you'll be able to sit down and watch the full movie just as it should have been filmed. Come back, get one of your Grandpa's plays, go back through that door and watch the play the way it was meant to be. You have eternity, so you can spend a day here watching a whole lot of movies and plays. Your family has so many forms of entertainment in this room, you'll be thankful that God gives you that eternity. Gosh, you remember all those songs you wrote and how you envisioned the music videos for them? Take your songs with you into that room and see exactly how each video would have been. Or you can take your PIP book that Jesus gave you and watch the many wonderful stories of your life the way they came to be."

"Wow! Oh, this IS SO Heaven, Chris. I hardly know where to begin with all this. Man, the ideas are flying through my mind and I don't know how to start."

"Just remember Andy, time has no value here. Why not start with those planets Jesus was telling you about?"

"You're right, Chris. But I might need a lot of paper and pencils to write down everything."

"No you won't. Remember when you worked on computers on the other side? Every time you came to a web site that you really liked, you just saved it in your favorites."

I am wigging out with excitement "Yeah… can I do that over here?"

"Sure. Our system is even better. As you're going through a book and see something that you'd like to save, just point to it, put your hand over your heart and say, save... it's saved for you. Over there by your family room - you see that big thing that looks like a Finder?"

"Yeah."

"It's like a Finder only it sets up your favorites. When you are done, you go over to your Favorites Finder and there is a keyboard. Push any key and a screen pops up on the surface. It asks you what topic ... you point to science ... it pulls up all the saves from that section... you point to the planet Jesus told you about and it pulls up everything you wanted saved about it. You can even plan out a fantasy on it if you want. You can fill in the names you want at the top ... complete the sentence, TODAY I AM GOING TO .... and then just save it to your fantasy file. Any day you're not sure what you want to do, just come in here and look in your fantasy file and you can print out any one you want."

"How cool is that?"

"Very cool ... and you can even look up stuff before you go to the Finders.... you just point to the search button .... then you put your hand over your heart and other hand on the screen .... then concentrate on the place you saw on TV a long time ago that looked like a fun place to go ... as your thinking about it, a picture will pop up on the screen - if it's what you're thinking of, you point to yes and it gives you all the info you need ... then you go over to the Finder in the Destinations section and you know exactly what you want it to find for you. It really cuts back on the smacking to be sure."

    Boy, I never imagined that the Resource Center would be that fascinating. I'm thinking this is going to be one of my longest days ever by the time I get through here. But then again, Chris keeps reminding me how time has no place on this side. I don't have to explore everything at once. I'm thinking I'll go over to the science area and look up those planets that Jesus told me about. After all, he is the Savior of all mankind and he did make the suggestion. It would really be uncool if I spent a lot of time watching Dad's movies before I finally got around to Jesu's planets. I'm sure Dad would understand that reasoning, I'm thinking, so I'm off to the science area.

    I stand and stare at the Finder. Somehow I have the feeling that it's going to smack me the first time just to mock me. You can never trust anyone connected to the science field, you know. I concentrate .... I want to check out the planets that Jesus, the Savior of all mankind told me to, Please .... I put my hand over my heart .... I extend my hand towards the surface of the Finder .... I want to check out the planets that Jesus, the Savior of all mankind told me to, please. My eyes closed, I touch the surface of the Finder and quickly jump out of the way. I slowly open my eyes and look around ... nothing. Suddenly, I notice in the distance a blinking light. I perk up. I start towards the blinking light - stepping very wide - away from the Finder that I still don't trust. As I get to the blinking light, I notice it is not a blinking light but a blinking book.

"Cool!"

I take the book from the shelf. "The Two Planets That Jesus, Savior of all mankind Thinks Andy Smith Might Like To Visit" .... good title. I take the book and find a seat at the table. Chris is back in his office and I truly have the place to myself.

I start reading through my book. Wow. The first planet is named Gurtz and seems to be full of nature. It's like a planet with nothing but Yellowstone Park on it. Lots of animals, some I'm familiar with, others I have never seen before. Pages of mountains with snow and deserts with playful dunes. Beautiful beaches and valleys. Beautiful scenery that seems endless. There doesn't appear to be any man-made stuff. No cities, cars, planes ... just nature. But I did find a huge hotel nestled in the middle of it all. Wow. What a great get away place for a family reunion, I think. I put my hand over my heart and point to the picture of this hotel and say - Save - and continue on. I stop at the ocean pictures and notice the same hotel sitting by the beaches. Hmmm. I think I'm picking up on the idea here. Maybe these books are written by your heart and are just there to show you the possibilities as you plan your fantasies.

Well Gurtz was interesting and frankly quite obviously being that it was recommended by Jesus the Savior of all mankind after all. I flip the page and come to my second planet, Bork.

Now Bork is kind of an odd place. There are all kinds of creatures busily going about. The pictures seem like a scene out of Star Wars or something. Lots of weird creatures, buildings and activity. I'm curious after Gurtz, why Jesus would recommend this one. I start reading some of the captions and as I do I start to become quite attracted to the place. It seems that with all these different creatures, the only common thread between them is, what I'm being told, a wonderful sense of humor. A Planet that specializes in a great sense of humor between all species of animals. Well I've always been a sucker for people with a good sense of humor

... and frankly, I'm tickled to think that this planet would be one of the first ones recommended to me by Jesus, the Savior of all mankind! But after my breakfast with him, I'm not completely surprised. You don't become the Savior of all mankind without a pretty healthy sense of humor, I'm thinking.

This is great. And the last part of the book gives brief samples of many other planets out there under the heading of "If you think Gurtz and Bork are cool, you're going to also like" and sure enough, I'm anxious to check many of them out as well.

But for now, I'm feeling a bit run out of gas. I'm thinking I've got enough information to encourage me to make the Resource Center a standard stop in my eternity planning.

As I head back to my room, I'm thinking about all the possible fantasies I could have on Gurtz alone ... and Bork ... and all the plays, movies, music videos and possibilities that exists just in my family room.

As I get to my door, I hear a snapping pop that shakes me as I bolt around to see what happened. I look around and am still alone. Then it occurs to me .... I'm guessing Dad, Hermes and Grandpa are planning something else and they just got a bit carried away with their talking while standing at a Finder. I start to laugh as I head to my bed. I'm thinking my Family Tree Resource Center probably has the highest electric bill in all eternity. God, I love this place.

Day Seven

After all that has happened to me this past six days, I wake up this morning thinking today I'm going to have a day off. I've learned so much in every adventure and I really feel the need to take a break and simply enjoy a day to myself. Of course, it's not hard to guess where that will be... I'm going to spend my day surfing on a nice beach in Hawaii!

I get up and am happy to see no blinking messages. I take my sheet and simply write .... TODAY, I'M GOING TO spend the day surfing on a beautiful beach in Hawaii.

I head to the door, open it and am standing before the most beautiful sight - next to my girls – I've ever seen. It's a gorgeous day with the sun peeking up from the Pacific blue waters. I go and find my lounge chair nicely laid out with a beach blanket laying over it. Next to the lounge is the perfect surfboard for me ... the right size and width for my tastes. Behind the surfboard is a beautiful resort and a outside bar that I am certain will keep those umbrella drinks I enjoy so much coming.

I stand there taking it all in. I think of how God made all the Heavens and the Earth in six days and on the seventh day he rested ... let there be no doubt - this is exactly where God would want to spend that seventh day!

I look out at the ocean. The waves are perfect. There seems to be little wind spray and I see no signs of any rip currents. The waves seem to be yelling at me, "Can Andy come out and play?!" I smile and without hesitating, I grab my surfboard and head for the ocean where I spend a great time conquering the mighty waves one by one.

I realize that Chris was right - there are no consequences on this side. Even when I wipe out, I come up laughing and enjoying every moment of being tossed about by the victorious wave. I could do this forever, but for now, I'm thinking I want to go back in and simply lay around for a while with an umbrella drink or two.

As I lay on the beach lounge with my umbrella drink, I start to go over everything that I have learned this week.... coming through the wash to get all the negative out of my heart .... the family reunion and meeting all those wonderful people that I can now call family .... speaking Latin to my girls and learning how things work when you are with people from 'the other side' .... spending the day at grandpa's on W45th street in New York City .... the walks along the beaches ....my day at the Zoo with Rosemary who was having a tooth pulled ... the talks with Chris ... the breakfast with Jesus, the Savior of all mankind who likes his eggs sunny side up and thinks I have a pretty impressive PIP number ... the concert with my family and all my songs ... the drinks afterwards at the bar .... the day spent exploring and learning all the great things about the Resource Center.

Boy this has been a great week. When you're living on Earth, you always wonder how Heaven will be. Will you recognize others there? Will you remember your life on Earth? Will you be able to influence those you left behind? How can you find happiness in Heaven and have it still make sense?

I now have the answers to those questions, and though I am certain that there are many other questions that may come up after my first week in eternity, I'm beginning to see how this really can work. It's amazing really, how much it makes sense. You only live on Earth for a short while, but it's just enough time to put your heart of love through all the emotional cycles of living in a world of consequences and free wills. This is what builds the true foundation of a heart. When you come through the wash, all that negative stuff gets washed away and the love in your heart has all the character and strength that was developed in that imperfect world. And now here, you have an eternity to build on that foundation of love through all your fantasies created from the roots of love.

I'm thinking this is going to be a great eternity for me. I start to think of what I would like to do next. I have so many fantasies that I want to pursue. So many family members from generations past I want to spend time with. The girls, of course. I have some trips to far away galaxies to explore and that's with only ONE book out of the Resource Center so far! I want so bad to work with Dad, Grandpa and Hermes and explore all the creative possibilities that our hearts can create.

I'm beginning to think too much. I decide to just close my eyes and take in the beauty of the moment. I listen to the gentle crashing of the waves and take a sip from my delicious umbrella drink as I begin to empty out my thoughts and simply relax.

Meanwhile, back at the Resource Center, Chris is relaxing in his office flipping through the pages of another book when another Angel comes through the door. Chris looks up and smiles right away. He recognizes her.

"I was hoping you'd drop by soon. How are things going?"

"She came through the wash yesterday. She's with her Family Tree right now."

"How's she doing?"

"Great. She's got a strong heart and she was totally amazed when I explained everything to her."

Chris hesitates, "Did she ask about him?"

The Angel smiles even wider.... "Oh, yeah ... once she learned how this all works it was the first thing she asked about."

Chris perks up "Excellent! What did you tell her?"

"I told her this is Heaven and that it could be better than she ever imagined. Of course, she quickly changed the subject and started asking about other stuff, but I could see it in her eyes." The Angel pauses, "Do you think we should do it?"

Chris doesn't give the question much thought "Are you kidding?! We have an obligation to do it!"

"Well, ok ... where is he now?"

"He's on a beach in Hawaii ... it would be perfect."

"Are you sure he'll be ok with it?"

"Are you kidding me? He's been avoiding that fantasy since he got here. If we don't force the issue with him, he'll never get around to it on his own. Trust me, He's going to be ok with this one."

They both smile. The Angel gets the right settings

from Chris and heads out the door. Chris sits back in his chair with a grin so wide and warm you sense he is about to explode with celebration.

Back at the beach, I'm embracing my day off the way it should be embraced. I'm in no hurry to do anything. I just want to lay with my eyes closed and my umbrella drink close by and soak in every feature of this beautiful setting.

"Mind if I join you?"

I freeze. My heart stops and soars at the same time. I know that voice without opening my eyes. And it's saying the words I have wanted to hear for so long. All I can do is smile like I have never smiled before. Now there is no doubt that I truly am in Heaven.

Day Eight

a bonus day

Day Eight

This eternity thing has really been exciting and clearly the hardest part is trying to keep your mind from exploding. Your mind is racing at 100 miles per hour thinking of the many ways you can spend a day. You constantly have to remind yourself that there is no time frame on this side. Eventually, I'll learn to relax and just go with my impulse when I get up every day, knowing whatever it is I choose to do can go as long as I want it to go without ever affecting any future fantasies. But with my creative mind racing as it is, I'm guessing that is easier said than done. At least in my case.

There is one part of all this that troubles me a bit. I know that when I came to this side I went through the wash and only the love came through. That's fine and makes sense, but I also can't help but think that many of our successes in the past are magnified because of the struggles and disappointments that preceded it. As a writer on the other side, I remember those few moments when I had success that the celebration wasn't just in getting something published, but more that I persevered through all the rejections and disappointments and didn't give up. That was as much the celebration as the actual story being published. If only the positives get through the wash, how can our successes ever be as meaningful or satisfying on this side if there are no references to the feelings of struggles and disappointments that lead up to that success?

I'm sure I'll figure that one out and I am very confident that God knows what He is doing on this side. I am in no way suggesting that I have come up with a flaw that God hasn't thought about. If I have learned anything these past seven days, it's that I don't know squat about how this side works, so I'm going to shut up about it and trust that the answer will present itself in due time.

So today I'm thinking I might spend some time in the Resource Center and develop some solid ideas for future fantasies I want to take on. After all, it's not like I don't already have a million ideas flashing through my mind already so why not throw some logs on that fire and test the waters to see if there truly is no place for insanity on this side. That's just how I ride after all; never take the straight, safe path - push the envelope and see just how far the limitations can take me.

I walk by the message machine – no messages – and the *TODAY I'M GOING TO* ... form and head straight into the Resource Center, where of course I find Chris sitting at the table browsing a book he probably doesn't need to read because he already knows everything. I know he's been a great help to me understanding this new world of mine, but I've always been a guy who likes to explore things on my own. Sometimes I think the adventure is lost if everything is explained to you before you try it.

I look over and just like that, Chris is no longer there. I panic! I just killed my Guardian Angel by thinking! Holy Cow!!

I go to his office and nervously open the door... only to find Chris quietly sitting at his table reading the same book. He looks up at me and smiles.

"How'd you do that?" I ask, trying to catch my breath.

His smile turns into that look that without a word tells me that my question does not warrant any response from him.

"I thought you had some questions, but apparently you want to be left alone." He says with an innocent smile.

One of the hardest things for me to get use to on this side is the creepy way Chris knows what I'm thinking. It annoys me to realize that this is going to go on for eternity and with only positive love going through the wash, I'm a bit pissed off that I may well be thrown back through the wash because of all the homicidal thoughts creeping into my mind with this little angel constantly reading my mind.

"Relax, Andy. Remember; this is your eternity, not mine. Certainly I know what you are thinking, but my role is not to judge but to serve as a guide – to help answer those questions you might have. In many ways, I'm just like this book here. You're only going to find me in your Resource Center because that's all I really am – a resource for you just as this book. Full of information that can guide you and help you to develop the eternity that best fits your heart. The only difference is that I can talk to you and help you with suggestions based on my understanding of how you think and feel. You need to stop looking at me as a threat and start thinking of me as a valuable resource for you as you plan your eternity."

There is absolutely nothing worse than talking to someone who can innocently turn your homicidal thoughts into guilt.

"Well, that's just fine. So tell me how am I supposed to get through this day when my heart is racked with guilt? I'm sure not feeling the love that supposedly was the ONLY thing to come through the wash, pal!"

Chris smiles and gestures for me to sit down with eyes that tells me to shut up and take a deep breath.

"Andy, you're doing fine. You just have to give God more credit. You're not the first person to come through the wash, you know. It takes time to get the hang of this place. There are always questions and challenges when people come to this side. God doesn't expect people to get it right away. And He certainly understands that until a person fully understands the possibilities of this side and the resources available, there is going to be feelings of frustration and uncertainty .... And in your case, homicide, I suppose. It's all good Andy. Nobody is going to throw you back through the wash. You're here for eternity and once you get all these issues resolved, I have no doubt that your eternity is going to be a very positive, fulfilling experience for you."

I pause and let what Chris has said soak into my heart, realizing that I truly have been too hard on him and maybe I should look at him as a resource and not a threat.

"I'm sorry, Chris .... I guess a guy like me just takes a little longer to get it."

"Don't be hard on yourself. God likes your type... you have a very loving heart that certainly got you through the wash fairly easy... and you have that rebellious spirit that challenges everything. That's a great combination because once you do get it and really begin to tap into the possibilities, your eternity is going to be one great adventure after another. I am in no way offended by your feelings of homicide towards me," his smile almost breaks into laughter, "and I assure you that once you really get the hang of this place, you won't be seeing that much of me. I truly am just a resource for you here."

He pauses and lets me take this all in before he continues.

"I was sitting out in the Resource Center because I thought you had some questions about feelings and how success on this side might not be as rewarding because there are no failures."

"Well, you did say that nobody gets hurt on this side, but sometimes those hurts and disappointments are what make our successes so gratifying."

"You are absolutely right to question that, Andy. Certainly, getting 300 bucks for publishing an article isn't that exciting until you put the backdrop of disappointments and rejections with it. That makes perfect sense. But remember when you came through the wash and the guardian of the book of life told you that only the memories that had a positive outcome came through the wash? The outcome is the point to remember. Everything on this side must have a positive outcome. There is no question that many of those positive outcomes came at great expense to the heart. It's those struggles of disappointments and set backs that build character. And without a strong character, those positive outcomes really are shallow and meaningless.

"Your eternity is going to be very superficial without the struggles and heartaches needed to bring character to your successes. All those feelings and emotions are necessary to build a strong positive outcome. The positive outcome is what's really important here, but the road that brought that positive outcome is just as important."

I'm sitting up now and feeling somewhat excited at what Chris is saying. Once again, it totally makes sense and I'm actually thankful he can read my mind because I likely would have wandered around eternity trying to figure that out on my own and never succeeded to come up with that answer. And - once again - Chris has shown his mastery at turning my annoyance away from him and directing right back at me as I shake my head and listen to my conscience quietly whispering, "You're an idiot!"

"Remember Andy, to think of me as a resource for

you – just like this book, only my information is all about your life. Let me give you an example of what I can do for you."

"Say you wanted to spend a day capturing your success as a writer, but you are not sure where or what you want that fantasy to be. Remember, I have complete reference to everything you did in your past life. I can pinpoint every emotion you had and can direct you to the exact moment those feelings crossed your mind.

"You can come to me and say, 'Chris- I want to experience the feeling of success as a writer but I'm obviously not sure where to go'... I will know exactly what you are looking for and give you a number. You can go over to the Favorites Finder I told you about here in the Resource Center and enter that number. It will pull up a number of pictures with short captions for you to choose from. Each picture will be of a specific time in your life that you may or may not remember that could have been a real turning point for you as a writer but for whatever reason did not turn out so good. When you select the one you want, you can save it into your Fantasy File for future references, or select to play it now. Then you go through the door I told you about and watch the story unfold just as you wish. Your heart will dictate the fantasy, so it will go as long as you want it to. It can be a short fantasy just to feel that moment of success, or you can make it a lifetime that carries you through many other successes as a writer. It's your fantasy.

"That's why I'm here, Andy. You had so many wonderful fantasies during your life and there really is no way you can remember them all. I can direct you to every feeling you ever had and give you the opportunity to create a great fantasy with a positive outcome. It's just one more tool you have to create your eternity into an exciting and positive world."

Wow! This is so cool. The thought of going back to my life and being able to rewrite those many rejections and turn them into a positive outcome is exciting to say the least. Once again I'm reminded of why God established eternity on this side without end, which is redundant, I know, but I'm just a simple guy trying to wrap my mind around all this. I get up and am anxious to get into the Resource Center when I pause and turn to Chris.

"What's in it for God? I mean, this is really cool and all, but it really is a selfish world I live in here. What does God get out of me living out all my fantasies like this?"

"Are you kidding? God is Love ... you are the fuel

that makes the love strong. Every person who comes through the wash adds to the strength of the love that feeds God. With each fantasy you create, God's love grows stronger. With every person that comes through the wash and begins to create their own eternity, God's love grows stronger. God realized at the beginning that for love to be universal and pure, it also had to be selfish. You are just starting your eternity – obviously many of the fantasies you create now may appear self-centered, but as you go along, you will begin to develop more and more fantasies that reflect the pure love in your heart that got you through the wash. Pure love always starts out selfish, but if it's truly pure, it grows into a powerful, universal love that God needs to survive. You – and everyone else who come through the wash – are a vital part of God's plan. God is love and you are an important reason why that love remains so strong."

Double Wow! I am humbled by this answer Chris has given me. For the first time, I feel as if I truly am an important part of Heaven. I am motivated to create great fantasies that will strengthen God's love even more. I'm excited at the thought that my fantasies here in my own selfish little eternity is going to contribute to the hope of all those still living back in my past world. God IS love and I finally realize that I have an important role in keeping that love strong! WOW – that's some pretty powerful thinking there, but I'm starting to think that maybe for the first time, I actually get it!

As I start out the door, Chris finishes up, "You're doing fine Andy. I'm here if you need anything. Oh, and Andy, just remember that no matter how annoying I may get, you can never kill me – I'm an Angel." He smiles.

I laugh but am strangely not all that comforted by his comment.

The End

(So, what are your 1ˢᵗ seven days going to be like?)

Planning Your Heaven

Once you understand the rules of Heaven, you can go ahead and create your own days in Heaven. It's fun and remember: it's for eternity, so don't box yourself into a time mentality. Your days are based on your fantasies, so tap into all those dreams you dwelled on in your heart of hearts and let them take you to new adventures.

- Remember: only positive outcomes get through the wash. There are no sad endings and your fantasies will never have a negative outcome.
- There are no negative consequences in Heaven. Eat what you want, drink what you want – it's all for pleasure, without affecting your health.
- Your first day is always your Family Tree day, which not only gives you a good foundation of your roots, but helps to create a million opportunities for future fantasies. And remember- you retain everything on this side. You will not forget anyone's name or how they fit into your family, etc.

- If you have a fantasy with someone who is still living, your conversations have to be within their world not yours – when I tried to tell my girls about my family tree it came out garbled Latin to them because they have not experienced this side yet. You can only relate to them through experiences familiar to them on Earth.
- The love in your heart is connected to the hearts of those you left behind. Though you can not go to Earth and solve their problems, your Guardian Angel may leave a message for you to spend a day with someone so they can 'feel' your closeness – spending the day at the zoo with Rosemary helped her through her tough time.
- Anyone who has come through the wash can be a part of your fantasy. If you write their name at the top, you can converse with them freely (Babe Ruth after the game at Wrigley) or you can chose to just observe without anyone knowing you are there (watching the game anonymously)
- If you want to meet someone in the Resource Center to plan a future fantasy, you must write on your sheet

'in a non-fantasy setting' which automatically sends a message to that person to meet you and gives them full control of what they say and think.

- You can be any age you want in your fantasies up to the age of your death – my grandfather died when he was twenty five so he can never be any older. Age doesn't matter on this side, as well as family positions – my Mom may appear older than her Dad (my grandpa) because he died so young, but it's the love that makes everyone family so there is no need for family structure outside of knowing who is what relation to everyone else.

- Each Family Tree has their own Resource Center that contains every topic consistent within the family – my resource center was heavy on entertainment because there are a lot of writers within my family tree.

- When someone comes through the wash, all their relatives are updated with knowledge of everything to that date – when I came through the wash, even my most distant relatives became fully aware of all the technologies and advances from my time and all the books in the Resource Center are automatically updated to reflect the possibilities to that time.

- Your social number is based on your opportunities to influence others on Earth – if you are the Pope or President, your social number would be a 1 or 2, if you are born into a world where you have little or no opportunities to influence others, your social number would be a 10.

- Your PIP number is determined by adding up all the instances where you had a positive impact on people – those whom you smiled at or made a kind gesture that made them feel better, gets you one point each – those whom your comments, writings or gestures had a significant positive influence on others gets you two points each – and those whom you had an absolute influence in turning their life into a positive direction gets you three points each. You add up these influence numbers and multiply this number by your social number to get your PIP number.

Have fun with it and remember; your fantasies come from a strong foundation of love you created on Earth. You can have all the fantasies you want and there will never be a negative outcome... no one will ever get hurt.... No hearts will be broken. It will always be positive. So have a nice eternity!

Challenge

By reading this story, it is hoped that you are now sitting back thinking, "I know what my first seven days would be..." And being that I am a very generous person who wants everyone to have as much fun as I do, I'm going to toss out this challenge to you:

My Best Day In Heaven!

Go ahead and give me your best day in Heaven. You must follow the rules of Heaven set in this story, but otherwise let your heart take you on the journey. Every story we receive will be read and judged on how well you follow the rules of Heaven and how much we enjoyed the story. If we get enough really good stories to warrant a follow-up book (that's the point, after all) – and your story is one of the stories selected – of course you will be paid and we will contact you to get a good personal bio from you so you can get full credit for your story. Maybe I'll put it up on my web site. Be creative!

Have fun – and good luck!

Submissions go to:

www.TKRwriteNOW.com

In Subject line: Best Day in Heaven